Seasonal Crafts

Autumn

Gillian Chapman

RSVP

RAINTREE STECK-VAUGHN
PUBLISHERS

The Steck-Vaughn Company

Austin, Texas

Seasonal Crafts

Spring • Summer • Autumn • Winter

Published by Raintree Steck-Vaughn Publishers, an imprint of Steck-Vaughn Company

Printed in Italy. Bound in the United States.
1 2 3 4 5 6 7 8 9 0 02 01 00 99 98

Library of Congress Cataloging-in-Publication Data
Chapman, Gillian.
Autumn / Gillian Chapman.
     p.   cm.—(Seasonal crafts)
    Includes bibliographical references and index.
    Summary: Provides directions for creating crafts, including kites, masks, and puppets, for the autumn season and comments on its events and festivals
    ISBN 0-8172-4870-6
    1. Handicraft—Juvenile literature.
    2. Autumn—Juvenile literature.
    [1. Holiday decorations. 2. Handicraft. 3. Autumn.]
    I. Title.
    TT160.C4925 1998
    745.594'1—dc21   97-4061

Picture acknowledgments:
Bruce Coleman Ltd 4 (Jane Burton); Eye Ubiquitous 12 (Chris Bland); Galaxy Picture Library 28 (Robin Scagell); Sally and Richard Greenhill 20; Impact 22 (Peter Arkell); Photri 6; Tony Stone Worldwide 16 (J. F. Preedy), 24 (David Young Woolff), 26 (David Hiser); Wayland Picture Library 10; Zefa 8, 14, 18. All commissioned photography, including the cover pictures by Chris Fairclough. Props made by Gillian Chapman.

Contents

Words that are shown in **bold** are explained in the glossary on page 31.

Autumn Colors

△ *A gray squirrel gathers nuts for winter storage.*

Autumn is a season of much activity. It is the time to get ready for the winter months ahead. Some animals gather food and store it for winter. Some birds fly to warmer places. The days begin to get colder and shorter. Trees and plants lose their leaves and seeds, and these provide the beautiful colors of autumn.

Fruit and cereal crops are harvested in autumn. It is a season of **celebration**, when people give thanks for a good harvest.

Autumn Projects

Autumn seeds, leaves, and other natural materials make exciting collages. Collect them on a dry day, taking only those that have fallen to the ground. At home, arrange your collection on newspaper, allowing them to completely dry before starting work.

Paints and Glues

Poster and powder paints are ideal for most crafts, but thicker poster paint or ready-mixed paint is better for splattering and printing. Having different-sized paintbrushes is helpful, and felt pens are perfect for fine details.

Keep old brushes for gluing. Rubber cement will stick large collage materials, like leaves and thick cardboard. Use a glue stick for paper and thin cardboard.

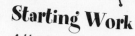

Starting Work

All the materials and equipment needed for each project are listed on each page. Ask an adult for help with cutting and gluing.

Recycling Materials

Many of the materials needed to make the projects in this book are free! Start to collect clean scrap paper, cardboard, and empty boxes—they all will be useful.

Use old newspapers and rags for covering work surfaces and for cleaning up. Plastic containers of all sizes are helpful for holding water and paint.

The Fall

Autumn is the time of the year when some types of trees lose their leaves and seeds. Sometimes the season is known as "Fall," because that is when leaves fall to the ground.

Leaves make sugar for the tree to feed on during the winter. On very cold, frosty nights the sugar cannot pass into the branches. It collects in the dying leaves, giving them their bright colors.

During the fall the colors of the trees change to reds, yellows, oranges, and browns. ▽

Making Splatter Prints

Autumn Gift Wrap

1 Cover the work surface with plenty of newspapers. Place a sheet of paper in the center and arrange the leaves on top.

2 Mix some thick paint and dip the toothbrush into it. Run an old pencil across the bristles, splattering paint over the paper and leaves. Let the paint dry before lifting off the leaves. △

You will need:

* Dry autumn leaves
* Newspapers
* Sheets of paper
* Construction paper
* Poster paints and brush
* Scissors and pencil
* Old toothbrush
* Old pencil or stick
* Scraps of ribbon

Autumn Leaf Cards

1 Place a leaf onto construction paper and draw around it. Then cut out the shape. ▽

2 Put the leaf shape on the newspaper and splatter it with paint. When the paint is dry, fold the leaf in half. Large leaves make attractive greeting cards. Thread the small ones with ribbon to make gift tags.

Chinese Kite Festival

The Chinese have been flying kites for thousands of years. The kites are usually made from light materials like bamboo, silk, and paper. The weathermen of Ancient China **forecasted** a wind from the east in early September. This made it a perfect time of year to hold a festival for kite flying.

On the last day of the festival, Chinese children have off from school to fly their kites. At the end of the day, they cut the kite strings and let them fly away.

Adults and children enjoy practicing kite flying in China. ▽

Making a Paper Kite

1 Position the three sticks across one another, as shown, and tie them together with string.

2 Place them on top of a sheet of paper cut to the same size as the stick framework. ▽

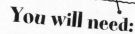

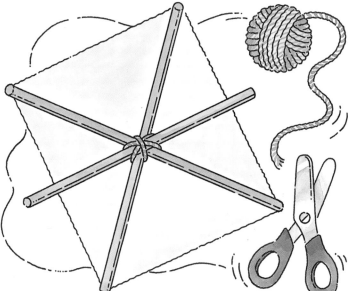

3 Using strips of tape, attach the paper to the sticks at the four corners. ▽

4 Turn the kite over and paint a scary face on the front.

5 Tie a long piece of string to the crossbar, and attach this line to the bamboo cane. You can fly the kite by holding the cane up high and running with the kite. ▽

9

Back to School

In many countries children go back to school at the beginning of autumn after the summer vacation. For most children it is the start of a new school year with new teachers, new topics, and new books and equipment.

Get ready for school with these two simple projects that use scraps of cardboard and construction paper. Make a bookmark to match the story you are reading, and clean up your desk with an animal letter holder.

Children at this school are all working together on a new project. ▽

Making Animal Bookmarks and Letter Holders

1 To make a bookmark, cut two slits in the cardboard. ▽

2 Cut some animal shapes and features from construction paper. Glue them to the top of the bookmark. ▽

1 To make a letter holder, cut off the top and sides of a cereal box. ▽

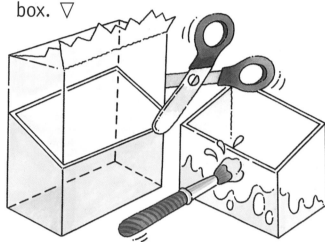

2 Paint the box and decorate it with scraps of colored cardboard cut into animal shapes. ▽

3 Slide the bookmark over the page in your book. Then you won't lose your place. △

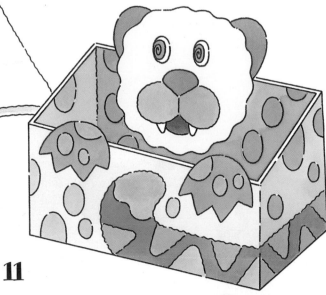

Harvest Time

△ *This French farmer will be celebrating a successful grape harvest.*

All around the world people celebrate the harvest and give thanks for good crops. A good grape harvest means a celebration in all countries that make wines. In Japan there is a rice harvest festival, and in West Africa the yam harvest is celebrated with dancing and mask making. In the United States, Thanksgiving is the holiday at the end of November celebrating the **colonists'** first successful harvest.

Some religions hold special harvest festivals of thanksgiving. Jewish families celebrate the end of harvest with the festival of **Succot**.

Making a Harvest Mask

You will need:
* Dry leaves, seeds, grasses, and twigs
* Dinner plate
* Cardboard
* Rubber cement
* Scissors and pencil
* Tape
* Wooden rod

1 Using a dinner plate as a pattern, cut a circle out of the cardboard. △

2 Hold the circle in front of your face and ask an adult to mark the position of your eyes and mouth. Then cut out the holes. (You may need an adult's help.) △

3 Tape a stick to the back of the mask so you can hold it. △

4 Cover the front of the mask with glue. Working from the outside, overlap leaves, grasses, and seeds until the mask is covered. ▽

13

Migration

Large numbers of birds do not stay in cold places for the winter. They **migrate** and fly thousands of miles to spend the winter in warmer places.

Swallows, wild ducks, and geese all migrate. They travel to the same place every year and return home in the spring to **breed**. The birds fly by day and night, possibly using the sun and stars as guides. Some insects, such as butterflies, also migrate.

A flock of geese fly across a beautiful autumn sky to find a warmer place for the winter. ▽

Making a Flapping Bird Mobile

You will need:
* 12-in. long wooden stick
* Colored cardboard
* Felt pens
* Scissors
* Tissue paper scraps
* Thread
* Hole punch

1 Cut out some bird shapes from the cardboard. Cut a slit in the birds' bodies and decorate the birds with felt pens. △

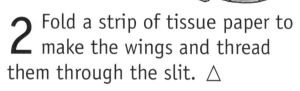

2 Fold a strip of tissue paper to make the wings and thread them through the slit. △

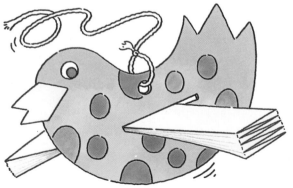

3 Punch a hole in each bird and tie a piece of thread through the hole. Tie the thread to the stick, making the birds hang at different heights. △

4 Tie a piece of thread to each end of the stick. Hang the mobile by an open window, and watch the birds fly in the breeze. ▽

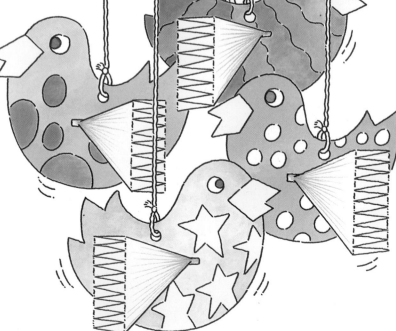

15

Hibernation

Autumn is a busy time for animals as they get ready for winter. They look for safe hiding places to store nuts and seeds. They build nests and grow thicker coats of fur. Frogs, lizards, and snakes bury themselves in underground holes away from the cold. Snails huddle together under stones.

Some animals, like bats, mice, and rabbits, **hibernate** through the winter. During the autumn they eat plenty of food to help them through the long months of rest. When animals hibernate their body temperatures fall, and their heartbeats are very slow.

A dormouse hibernates, safely curled up in a warm nest of dried grass. ▽

Making an Animal Pencil Holder

You will need:
* Cardboard tube
* Construction paper
* Poster board
* Scissors
* Glue stick
* Felt pens

1 Cover the cardboard tube with construction paper. Line up the top of the tube with the edge of the paper. Glue it in place. △

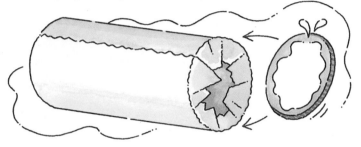

2 Tuck any extra paper into the bottom of the tube. Cut out a circle of cardboard, and glue it to the base of the tube. △

3 Cut out two identical animal shapes from the poster board. These will need to be large enough to glue halfway around the tube and to each other. △

4 Using the glue stick, glue the animal shapes in place. Decorate the pencil holder with scraps of construction paper and felt pens. ▽

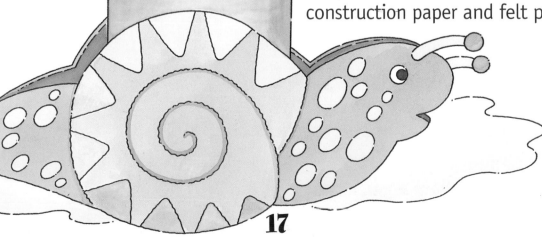

17

Autumn Animals

△ *The spotted brown feathers of this pin-tailed sandgrouse camouflage it among the dried leaves and grasses.*

In autumn the colors of the trees and plants change from greens to golden browns. Fallen leaves and seeds lie on the ground.

Animals and birds such as rabbits, pheasants, mice, and snakes are **camouflaged** by these autumn colors. The fur of some animals changes color when the season changes. In winter the mountain hare **molts**. Its brown summer fur changes to white so that the hare blends in with the snow around it.

Making a Camouflage Collage

You will need:
* Feathers, dry leaves, twigs, and seeds
* 2 pieces of cardboard
* Long box
* Glue
* Scissors
* Brown paint and brush

1 Glue the long box to the bottom edge of a piece of stiff cardboard. ▽

2 Paint the box brown and let it dry. Then make an autumn collage with the natural materials you have collected. Cover the cardboard, gluing the collage in place. ▽

3 Draw an animal shape on the other piece of cardboard and cut it out. Decorate the shape with the rest of the natural materials, gluing them to the cardboard. △

4 When the animal collage is dry, glue it to the front of the box. The collage will now stand up. The animal will be camouflaged by the background of natural materials. ▷

19

Diwali

The festival of Diwali is the beginning of the Hindu New Year. Hindus remember the ancient story of Rama and Sita, who were **banished** from their kingdom for fourteen years. Rama came back and killed the evil, ten-headed **demon** king, Ravana. Then Rama was made king.

Diwali means "row of lights," and Hindus place small oil lamps, called **divas**, in their windows to guide Rama and Sita home. Families celebrate Diwali by holding parties, watching fireworks, and giving presents.

Hindu families get together to celebrate Diwali, or the "Festival of Light." ▽

Making Festive Lanterns

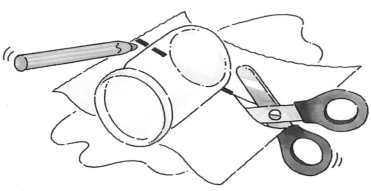

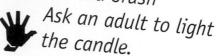

You will need:
* Clean jelly jar
* String
* Thin paper
* Pencil and scissors
* Hole punch
* Tape
* Paints and brush
  🖐 Ask an adult to light the candle.

1 Cut your sheet of paper to the same height and width as the jelly jar and cut off the rest. △

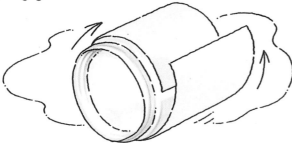

2 Wrap the paper around the jar to make sure it is long enough to cover it and allow for a 1 in. overlap. △

3 Paint patterns on the paper. When the paint dries, punch holes in the paper for the candle to shine through. ▽

4 Wrap the decorated paper around the jar and hold it in place with the tape. Tie a string handle to the rim of the jar. ◁

🖐 Ask an adult to place a candle in the jar and light it. NEVER leave lighted lanterns unattended!

21

United Nations Day

△ *By planting a tree, these children are helping to make their world a better place in which to live.*

The United Nations (UN) was formed on October 24, 1945. The world had been at war for more than five years, so the UN was created to help keep world peace. Every year on this day people think about peace around the world.

The UN organized The Earth Summit, held in 1992 in Rio de Janeiro. More than 150 governments agreed to a set of laws, called Agenda 21. These laws were made to help save our planet from war and **pollution** as we move into the next century.

Making a Peace Collage

1 Look through your collection of old magazines and comic books and cut out all the pictures that make you think of peace. ▽

You will need:
* Piece of poster board
* Old magazines
* Glue stick
* Scissors
* Pencil
* Construction paper

2 Arrange the pictures on the poster board. Glue them in place with the glue stick. △

3 Fold a piece of construction paper. Draw a simple outline of a person on the paper and cut it out. Make sure you cut through all the layers.

4 Carefully unfold the row of people. Cut out several more in different colors. Glue the people along the edge of your collage. They show people around the world joining together for peace.

Halloween

△ *On Halloween night children dress up ready for fun!*

Halloween is the night for dressing up and making mischief! Children sometimes go "trick or treating" with their friends.

Long ago, the **Celts** celebrated their New Year's Eve on this night with great feasts and dancing. They lit huge bonfires to frighten away the ghosts and evil spirits that they believed were **haunting** them.

This day was also made into a Christian festival and is known as the eve of All Hallow's, or All Saints', Day.

Making Scary Spiders

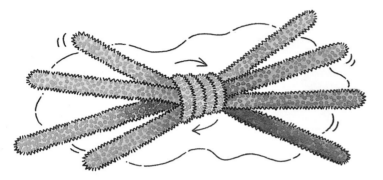

You will need:

For each spider:
* 4 black pipe cleaners
* Thin black cardboard
* Glue
* Scissors
* Fine black elastic
* Round white labels
* Black felt pen

1 Place four black pipe cleaners together and twist them in the center so they are secure. △

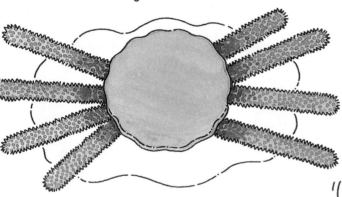

4 Stick two white labels onto the spider. Draw in the eyes with a black felt pen.

Make a whole family of scary spiders and hang them around the house for Halloween. ▽

2 Cut a circle out of the black cardboard, and glue it to the center of the pipe cleaners. △

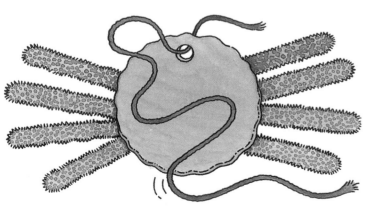

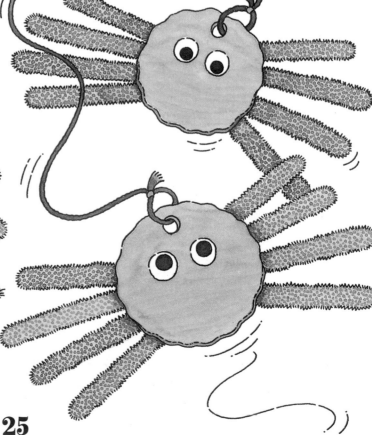

3 Make a small hole in the top of the cardboard. Then thread the black elastic through and tie it. △

All Souls' Day

△ *Mexicans make large skeleton puppets that dance in the Day of the Dead celebrations.*

On this day Christians remember their family members and friends who have died. Some people believe that on this day the souls return to Earth to visit their old homes.

In Mexico it is known as the Day of the Dead and is an important religious festival. People parade in the streets in colorful costumes and perform dances with masks. Mexican families leave cakes and flowers on the graves to welcome the souls back home on this special day.

Making a Skeleton Puppet

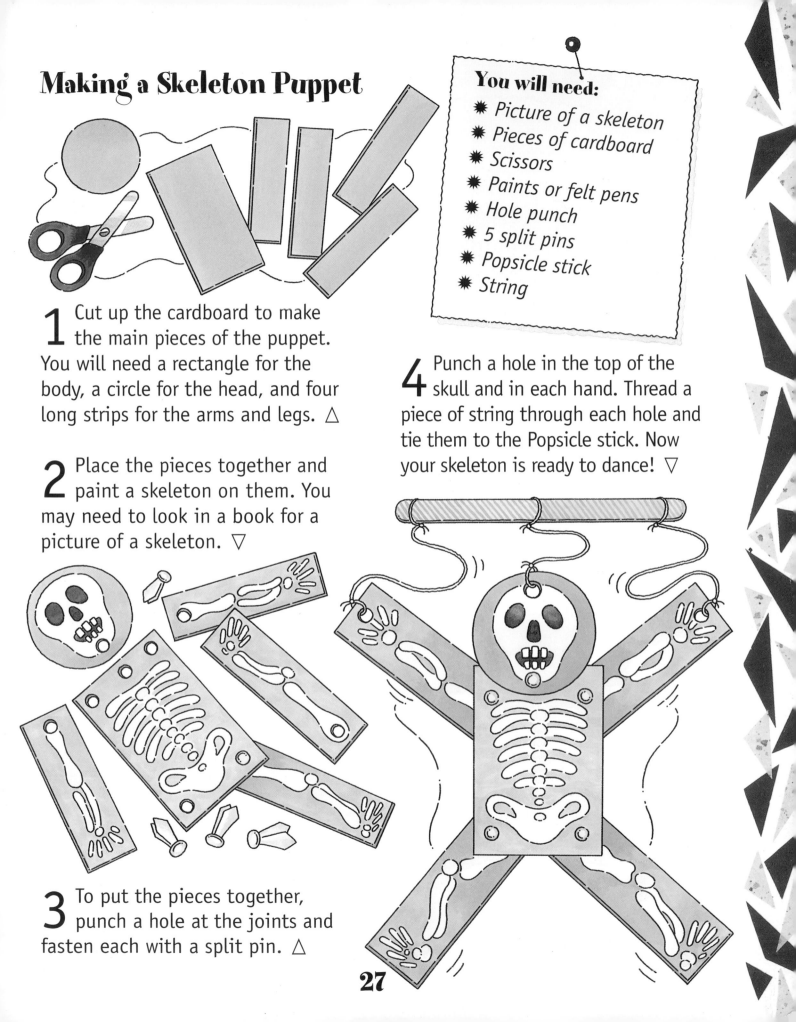

You will need:
* Picture of a skeleton
* Pieces of cardboard
* Scissors
* Paints or felt pens
* Hole punch
* 5 split pins
* Popsicle stick
* String

1 Cut up the cardboard to make the main pieces of the puppet. You will need a rectangle for the body, a circle for the head, and four long strips for the arms and legs. △

2 Place the pieces together and paint a skeleton on them. You may need to look in a book for a picture of a skeleton. ▽

4 Punch a hole in the top of the skull and in each hand. Thread a piece of string through each hole and tie them to the Popsicle stick. Now your skeleton is ready to dance! ▽

3 To put the pieces together, punch a hole at the joints and fasten each with a split pin. △

27

Autumn Stars

A clear autumn night is a good time to look at the stars. Groups of stars are called constellations. The Ancient Greeks saw groups of stars as pictures in the sky. They named these groups of stars after creatures or people from their **myths**.

One group of stars is called Ursa Major, which means "The Great Bear." Another is called Scorpius, the scorpion that stung **Orion** to death. Look in a book about the night sky to learn more about constellations.

A group of stars called the Big Dipper can be seen in the autumn sky. It is part of the Great Bear constellation. ▽

Making Star Cards

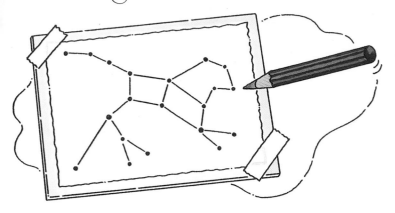

You will need:
* A book on constellations
* Piece of poster board
* Sharp pencil
* Tracing paper
* Drawing pin
* Paints or felt pens

1 Find a picture of a constellation in a book, and copy or trace it onto the poster board. △

3 Draw in the character or animal that the constellation represents, using the book as a guide. Keep the animal shape as an outline or color in the details. ▽

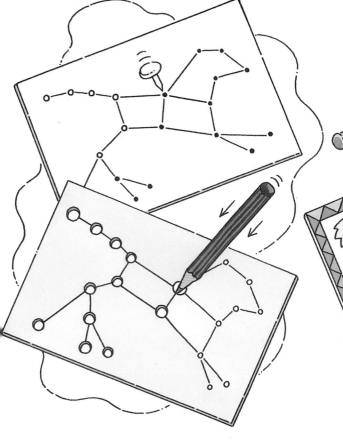

2 With an adult's help punch through the stars with a drawing pin. Then carefully enlarge the holes with a pencil. △

Hold the star card up to a light and watch the stars twinkle.

Autumn Calendar

This calendar refers only to events and festivals mentioned in this book.

Chinese Kite Festival
September 1–9
Rosh Hashanah (The Jewish New Year)
Late September/early October
Succot (The Jewish Feast of Tabernacles)
September or October
Harvest Time
Mid-October in Great Britain, U.S., and other Western countries
United Nations Day
Late October
Diwali (The Hindu Festival of Light)
October or early November
Halloween
October 31
All Saints' Day
November 1
All Souls' Day
November 2
Thanksgiving
Fourth Thursday of November

(Many religions and cultures use the lunar calendar, which means that their festivals are not held on the same day every year.)

Glossary

banished To be thrown out of a place against your will.

breed To give birth to young.

camouflaged To be hidden against a similar background.

Celts A group of people who lived in northern Europe.

celebration A special happy event or festival.

colonists A group of people who move and settle in a new land

demon A wicked being or spirit.

divas A Hindu word for small, clay oil lamps.

forecasted To have worked out what will happen in the future.

haunting Frightening and worrisome.

hibernate To spend the winter in a deep sleep.

migrate To move from one place to another, over a long distance.

molt When animals lose their fur coat or skin.

myths Stories from the past.

Orion A Roman god, who has a star constellation named after him.

pollution Spoiling the land, sea, or air by making it dirty.

Succot Festival that remembers the Jews' search for a homeland.

Further Reading

Jacobs, William J. *Search for Peace: The Story of the United Nations.* New York: Simon & Schuster Children's, 1994.

Murray, Peter. *How to Make Kites.* Umbrella Books. Plymouth, MN: Child's World, 1996.

Penney, Sue. *Hinduism.* Discovering Religions. Austin, TX: Raintree Steck-Vaughn, 1996.

Thompson, C. E. *Glow-in-the-Dark Constellations: A Field Guide for Young Stargazers.* New York: Putnam Publishing Group, 1989.

We Celebrate Harvest. Holidays and Festivals. New York: Crabtree Publishing, 1986.

Willis, Abigail. *Halloween Fun: Great Things to Make and Do.* New York: Kingfisher Books, 1993.

Index